CLB 1821
© 1988 Colour Library Books Ltd, Godalming, Surrey, England
All rights reserved
Color separation by Hong Kong Graphic Arts Limited, Hong Kong
Printed and bound in Barcelona, Spain by Cronion, S.A.
Published 1988 by Crescent Books, distributed by Crown Publishers, Inc.
ISBN 0 517 64457 6
h g f e d c b a

THE SHAKERS

Text by
L. Edward Purcell

CRESCENT BOOKS
NEW YORK

A GUIDE TO SHAKER SITES, MUSEUMS AND COLLECTIONS

Original Shaker Villages

The eight remaining original Shaker villages open to visitors vary considerably in their levels of preservation, interpretation, and programming, but all offer worthwhile experiences for anyone interested in the Shakers.

The first formal Shaker settlement was **Mt. Lebanon Shaker Village, N.Y.,** located on highways 20 and 22, between Albany, N.Y., and Pittsfield, Mass., near the state borders. Between 1787 and 1947, this was the center of the Shaker Ministry, which directed policy for Shakers nationwide, and one of the largest Shaker villages. Most of the buildings are now used by a private prep school, but several, including the Second Meeting House with its unusual arched roof, are open from July 1 until Labor Day. Admission: $3.00 for adults, $1.50 for children and students. More information: Mt. Lebanon Shaker Village, Shaker Rd., New Lebanon, NY 12125 (518) 794-9500.

Just north of Albany, N.Y., next to the Albany County Airport off 1-87 (Adirondack Northway), is the remaining portion of the **Watervliet** Shaker settlement, first occupied by Mother Ann and her first followers when it was called Niskeyuna. Her grave in the Watervliet Cemetery, along with the Meeting House, may be visited. The original village, which lasted from 1787 until 1938, is now under development. Special programs include a Shaker Learning Fair and a Public Day in May. Open year-round, Tuesday through Thursday 9-3, Friday 9-12, or by appointment. Admission is charged for guided tours. More information: Shaker Heritage Society, Trustees Office, Albany-Shaker Road, Albany, NY 12211 (518) 456-7890.

Hancock Shaker Village, Mass. is probably the best-known and most popular Shaker tourist site in New England, symbolized by the photogenic Round Stone Barn. The village is close by the Berkshires at the junction of highways 20 and 41, five miles west of Pittsfield, Mass. (note that it cannot be reached from the north by highway 43, travelers must use route 20 to the south). The settlement was gathered in 1790, and the last Shakers left in 1960. The site was immediately taken over by a restoration group and now offers visitors a superb view of the Shaker past. The entire village is an outdoor living-history museum, filled with interesting buildings (18 open for tours), exhibits, and demonstrations. There are special programs throughout the year, including crafts and industries, a kitchen festival, children's tours, basketmaking, woodworking, herb culture, weaving, ironworking, singing, and antiques. Lunch is available at a restaurant at the visitors' center. Open daily 9:30-5:00 from Memorial Day through October 31, with additional special events. Admission: $6.00 for adults, $2.00 for children 6-12, children under 6 free. Special rates for senior citizens, students, families, and groups. More information: Hancock Shaker Village, P.O. Box 898, Pittsfield, MA 01202 (413) 443-0188.

The **Enfield, N.H.** Shaker settlement on the shores of Mascoma Lake on highway 4A (off 1-89 east of Hanover) features the magnificent Great Stone Dwelling, the largest Shaker dwelling in the country. There are a dozen buildings on the walking tour, plus a museum and gift shop. Special programs on antiques and other topics during the summer. Museum open daily 10:00-4:00 (closed Thurs.) from June 21 to mid-October, weekends only October-May. Admission: $3.50 adults, $2.50 seniors and children, $1.00 Children 6-11, children under 6 free. Group rates available. More information: Lower Shaker Village Museum, Enfield, N.H. 03748 (603) 632-5533.

Canterbury Shaker Village, N.H. is one of two remaining active Shaker communities, with a few elderly shaker sisters forming a remnant of the settlement which began in 1792. Most of the village is now a museum, with guided tours of six of the 22 buildings, craft demonstrations, and Shaker-style meals available for visitors. Located north of Concord, off 1-93, the village has been an important center for Shaker culture since its founding, and shows the adaptions of Shakers to modern life. Special lectures, seminars, and workshops are offered. Open 10:00-5:00 Tuesday through Saturday from mid-May to mid-October. Admission: $4.50 adults, $1.75 children 6-12. More information: Shaker Village, Inc., Canterbury, N.H. 03224 (603) 783-9977.

Sabbathday Lake, Maine is home to the handful of Shaker brothers and sisters who form the United Society of Shakers. They operate a farm and a research center and still practice Shaker ways and worship. Much of the village is open to visitors, however, and many buildings are undergoing restoration. One of the interesting experiences is public worship at the Meeting House on Sundays. Located at Poland Spring on highway 26, off the Maine Turnpike betwen Gary and Auburn. Open 10:00-4:30 Tuesday through Saturday between Memorial Day and Columbus Day. Admission: $2.50 adults, $1.75 children, children under 6 free. Walking tours: $3.50 adults, $2.00 children, children under 6 free. Group rates available. More information: The United Society of Shakers, Sabbathday Lake, Poland Spring, ME 04274 (207) 926-4391.

Of all the Shaker sites, **Shakertown at Pleasant Hill, Ky.,** offers the fullest range of experiences for the visitor, including overnight lodging in Shaker buildings and superb, 19th-century-style meals in the former Trustees Office. One of the large western Shaker settlements, Pleasant Hill was founded in 1806 and was closed by the Shakers in 1910. The restoration began in 1961 and resulted in a beautifully conceived and executed living museum of Shakerdom and 19th-century agricultural life.

Twenty-seven buildings are on the self-guided tour, with interpreters and craftsmen sprinkled about for explanation and demonstration. Many special events throughout the year, including music, dancing, special teas, crafts, lectures, Winter Weekends, and Shaker Heritage Weekends. Also overnight conference facilities and paddle-wheel excursions on the Kentucky River. Located on highway 68 south of Lexington, near Harrodsburg. Open year-round except Christmas Eve and Christmas Day. Reservations needed for lodging and dining. Admission: $4.00 adults, $2.00 children 12 through high school, $1.00 children under 11. Group rates available. More information and reservations: Shakertown at Pleasant Hill, Rt. 4, Harrodsburg, KY., 40330 (606) 734-5411.

Shakertown at South Union, Ky., was a long-lived Western Shaker village, closing in 1922. Six original buildings remain, with a museum in the Centre Family Dwelling. Restoration of more buildings is currently underway. A late Shaker building (1917) is now an antique mall and post office. A Shaker Festival in July features crafts, meals, tours, and an outdoor drama. Located on highways 68 and 80, between Bowling Green and Auburn, Ky. Museum open 9:00-5:00 daily and 1:00-5:00 Sundays May 1 to October 1. Admission: $2.00 adults, $1.00 Children 6-12, children under 6 free. Group rates available. Shaker Tavern Restaurant open Wednesday-Saturday evenings and Sunday noon. More information: Shakertown, South Union, KY 42283 (502) 542-4167.

Museums, Exhibits, and Collections

Many interesting Shaker artifacts (especially furniture) and documents are to be found in other museums and special collections. These are not original Shaker sites, but several are located close to former Shaker settlements.

The **Shaker Museum at Old Chatham, N.Y.,** is probably the most comprehensive collection of Shaker material in the country, including more than 32,000 objects (half on display) and thousands of manuscripts, books, documents, and photographs. Visitors may tour Shaker displays exhibited in re-created Shaker settings, with material from all Shaker settlements and covering the entire span of Shaker history. While not an actual Shaker site, the museum at Old Chatham gives perhaps the best overall interpretation of Shakers in America. Located one mile south of Old Chatham, N.Y., off County Road 13. Exhibits open daily 10:00-5:00 May 1 through October 1, library open weekdays year round. Admission: free to members, $3.50 adults, $3.00 seniors, $2.50 ages 15-21, $1.50 ages 6-14, young children free. More information: The Shaker Museum, Shaker Museum Road, Old Chatham, NY 12136 (518) 794-9100.

A Shaker building and displays from the Harvard, Mass., village share the spotlight at the **Fruitlands Museum** with displays on the Transcendentalists. Located in Harvard, Mass. Open 1:00-5:00 Tuesday through Sunday, May 30-September 30, plus October weekends. Admission: $3.00 adults, $.50 children ages 7-16, children under 6 free. More information: Fruitlands Museum, Prospect Hill Road, Harvard, MA 01451 (617) 456-3924.

The **Shelburne Museum,** on highway 7 south of Burlington, has a Shaker building and furniture from Canterbury, N.H. More information: Shelburne Museum, Burlington, VT 05482 (802) 985-3344.

The **Kentucky Museum** at Western Kentucky University in Bowling Green, near the site of the Shaker village at South Union, has Shaker furniture and artifacts but is most important for its collection of original documents and books on Shakers. More information: The Kentucky Museum, WKU, Bowling Green, KY 42101 (502) 745-2592.

The planned Cleveland suburb of Shaker Heights, Ohio, was built on top of the completely obliterated site of North Union, the largest of the Western Shaker settlements. The current **Shaker Historical Society's** museum and collection commemorate the village. More information: Shaker Historical Society, 16740 South Park Blvd., Shaker heights, OH 44120 (216) 921-1201.

The Historical Library of the **Western Reserve Historical Society** in Cleveland, Ohio, is the largest single collection of research material on the Shakers, including much from official Shaker archives. A museum includes Shaker objects. More information: The Western Reserve Historical Society, 10825 East Blvd., Cleveland, OH 44106 (216) 721-5722.

The several important Shaker villages in western Ohio are remembered by collections and activities in the Dayton-Lebanon area. **The Warren County Historical Society Museum** in Lebanon, Ohio, (between 1-71 and 1-75 on highway 63) has displays focused on Union Village, a large Western Shaker settlement. Open daily except Mondays. Admission: $2.00 adults, $1.00 students. More information: Warren County Historical Society Museum, 105 South Broadway, Lebanon, OH 45036 (513) 932-1817.

Also in Lebanon, the **Golden Lamb** inn, famed for its cuisine and historically furnished rooms, features displays of Shaker material. More information: The Golden Lamb, 27 South Broadway, Lebanon, OH 45036 (513) 932-5064.

In the Dayton suburb of Kettering, Ohio, is the **Kettering-Moraine Museum and Historical Society,** whose collecting and publishing interests center on the Shaker village at Watervliet, Ohio. More information: Kettering-Moraine Museum and Historical Society, 35 Moraine Circle, South Kettering, Ohio 45439 (513) 299-2722.

The **Winterthur Museum** in Delaware counts many Shaker items among its magnificent collections and displays of decorative arts, plus the library's Edward Deming Andrews Memorial Shaker Collection. More information: The Henry Francis du Pont Winterthur Museum, Winterthur, DE 19735 (302) 656-8591.

Note: All times, dates, and prices are listed as current at the time of publication. They are subject to change and visitors should contact specific sites or museums for up-to-date information.

When first coming upon a Shaker village, it is hard to be unmoved. The pleasing proportions of the buildings, the orderly plan of the grounds, and the simple beauty of every artifact and tool conspire to give even the most casual tourist a sense of Shaker harmony – a feeling that the Shakers achieved in their day a grace and unity of spirit we would give much to recover.

The price, however, of Shaker harmony would be great for most modern people. Perhaps only the handful of living Shakers, most of them elderly women, have insight in to the qualities of spirit and mind required to live the Shaker life. For, while the Shakers produced admirable things that retain their magic across the years, Shaker beliefs and lifestyles belong for the most part to an earlier time, when simplicity and perfection seemed more possible to attain.

Two hundred years ago, when Shakerism was imported to America during the Revolution, the doctrines and practices of the tiny sect were strange and even frightening. As the Shakers attracted adherents, grew in numbers, and spread from New England into Ohio and Kentucky, their very success seemed to defuse the threat, and the Shakers came to be reasonably well tolerated by the "world," as they called non-believers. Tolerance was not the same thing as conversion, however, and by the turn of the century Shakerism was in a steep, deadly decline.

Yet not even the most devout believer during the Shaker heyday might have foreseen the widespread modern interest in Shaker ways and Shaker objects.

Today, restored Shaker villages and Shaker museums attract hundreds of thousands of visitors. Authentic Shaker furniture commands unholy prices. Shaker songs have worked their way into the fabric of both classical and popular music. And, writings on every detail about the Shakers fill page after page and shelf after shelf.

Shakerism arose in one of the more grimy corners of 18th-century England. The textile-producing city of Manchester in the late 1700s was, for the poorer folk, a nasty, brutish place, undergoing economic changes that outstripped society's ability to care for the unskilled and the unpropertied.

Among these was a women named Ann Lees, born in 1736 to an impoverished home life that was little improved by a teenage marriage to John Standen, a blacksmith. Her health was early broken by several pregnancies and painful miscarriages, and her worldly prospects were bleak.

Ann was deeply spiritual by nature, and like many others in England and the American colonies, yearned for salvation and positive signs that she could be saved by faith from the depressing travail of her day-to-day life. She was attracted to meetings in the home of a Quaker couple, where the participants were seized by a religious fervor that expressed itself through fits of shaking and violent behavior.

She soon assumed the lead of the small group of frenzied worshippers and began to preach in public, loudly criticizing organized religion. Since church and state were one in England, her activities attracted the notice of the civil authorities, and she was thrown in jail for disturbing the peace.

When Ann emerged from her cell, she told her companions of a wonderful visitation by Jesus himself, with whom she was henceforth to be united as the feminine side of God on Earth, a new manifestation of the Messiah – Jesus Christ the male and Mother Ann the female. She also announced a set of precepts that would free adherents from sin forever: confession, celibacy, and perfection of life.

Ann soon gathered her handful of followers and, like other dissident religionists before her, embarked for the New World. After a hazardous voyage, during which their sinking ship seemed to have been saved by a miracle, the group landed in New York City, where they split up in search of work. Ann could do no better than a part-time job as a housekeeper and, after being abandoned by her husband (who, oddly enough, had accompanied her to America) she nearly starved in an attic hovel. Clearly the city held no promise for Ann and her co-believers.

In 1776, Ann and her small band moved to upstate New York, to a swampy section of land near Albany, called by its Indian name, Niskeyuna (later re-named Watervliet). Economic conditions were scarcely better than in New York City, but the believers survived and scratched out a toe-hold in the rough country. Gradually, other religious seekers in the area began to come to listen to Ann and the "Shaking Quakers," who told of a certain path to salvation and peace of mind.

Upper New York State and most of rural New England were then in the grip of a prolonged and red-hot religious revival. Wave after wave of enthusiasm had swept the region, spawning pockets of new belief and splintering old-line denominations. Whatever the sources of the

Great Revival, the result was a widespread, popular religious revolt that particularly captured the poorer classes and the working people. Thousands sought certainty amidst the fervid confusion of revivalism. They prized intense expression of belief, and at the same time they wanted clear instructions on how to escape from a life of sin.

Mother Ann and her Shakers offered both. During worship they were seized by the power of the Spirit and whirled, turned, shook, prophesied, and spoke in unintelligible tongues. Their services, they believed, reflected the practice of the primitive Christian Church, now renewed by the vigor of the Second Coming in Mother Ann. Yet, side by side with the expressions of extreme religious emotion, the Shakers soberly laid out a rule of life that guaranteed salvation. Follow the guidelines – stern though they be – and you were certain of attaining grace. For many, especially those filled with confused religious longing, these messages were powerful and compelling.

Exhausted by a hazardous two-year mission through Massachusetts, New York, and Connecticut, Mother Ann died at Niskeyuna in 1784, but she had anointed a line of successors who, within a few years, attracted hundreds of converts and began a process of codifying the Shaker doctrine and practice. Shaker societies formed at New Lebanon, New York; Hancock, Tyringham, Harvard, and Shirley in Massachusetts; Canterbury and Enfield, New Hampshire; Enfield, Connecticut; and Alfred and Sabbathday Lake (New Glouster), Maine.

It became clear to the early Shaker leaders that in order to lead perfect lives and avoid contamination by the world it was necessary to dwell separately. Under the leadership of Joseph Meacham, the growing sect began to "gather" in distinct settlements, typically situated on large farms donated by prosperous converts. Moreover, all Shakers were to share and share alike in the new "Gospel Order." When a new convert pledged fealty to the Shaker covenant (at first verbal but later a written agreement), all unencumbered property and goods were signed over to the communal body. All believers in the community were to put hands and hearts to work for the sealing of their corporate and individual salvation.

This set of ideas – belief in the second coming, separatism, communal life – was fairly common intellectual coin at the beginning of the 19th century. Many others besides the Shakers fastened on similar notions (sometimes without the religious element) and sought to establish communities where the trials of everyday life would vanish. Most of these experiments failed in short order. The Shakers prospered.

Not without difficulty, however. The early Shakers had to establish their eleven New-England communities in the face of considerable resistance. Mother Ann's two-year mission, for example, included a long series of encounters with hostile mobs, who beat up Shaker men and hounded Shaker women out of town. Part of the early hostility was based on patriotic suspicion of a group of Britons who wandered the countryside preaching pacifism during the Revolutionary War, but in a more fundamental way, the Shakers were perceived as a threat to the established social, religious, and economic order. By setting themselves apart, declaring their superiority, and eliminating private property, the Shakers cut at much of what the rest of the world held to be valuable.

In addition, the insistence on celibacy touched raw nerves. Apparently, few among their opponents believed the Shakers' claim to sexual abstinence, and they charged the sect with sexual perversion and orgiastic deviations, including castration of male converts and murder of illegitimate babies. The available evidence says that most Shakers truly lived with their belief that the sexes should remain entirely separate, but their rigid insistence on breaking down one of the most fundamental human relationships won them few friends among the skeptics.

Eventually, however, the orderliness and sobriety of Shaker life (apart from the extremes of worship) did much to defuse the violent opposition and, as the number of believers gathered into Shaker settlements grew, they avoided problems by strict attention to business and cooperation with their neighbors.

In 1805, the New-England Shakers looked to the frontiers of Ohio and Kentucky. Missionaries dispatched westward found fertile ground – particularly in Kentucky, where a replay of the previous eastern revivals had raged for several years, preparing the way for the Shaker message. Within the next 20 years, large and prosperous Shaker societies came into being at North Union (near Cleveland), Union Village, Watervliet (near Dayton), and Whitewater in Ohio, and at Pleasant Hill and South Union in Kentucky. In 1836, reshuffling

of members created a village at Groveland, New York.

Within these Shaker societies all was order. Every member had a place in the structure and a set of duties. At the top were the Elders and Eldresses (usually two and two) who had overall charge of everyone and everything in the society. There were also appointed Deacons and Deaconesses who dealt with day-to-day temporal affairs, and later, Trustees who handled business with the outside world. In keeping with the Shaker belief in equality of the sexes, men and women shared in authority and duty.

The entire body of Shakerdom was guided by the wisdom of the elders at New Lebanon – a group known as the "Ministry." Yet each settlement, for the most part, ran its own affairs. Within the separate villages, there were further divisions into "families," comprised of about 50 believers with equal numbers of men and women. At the physical and spiritual heart were the most committed Shakers of the Center or Church Family. Outward were formed other families, usually comprised of newer converts who seemed as yet less sanctified.

Men and women, although working and worshipping side by side, lived strictly separate lives. Even casual conversations between the sexes were forbidden. Shaker buildings were constructed with double doorways and stairs so no physical contact could occur during comings and goings. The men undertook the heavier work of farming and building and the women rotated domestic duties such as cleaning and cooking, although they shared with the men in the manufacture of goods for sale.

Everyone within a Shaker society was dedicated to work. This was the central theme of daily life and represented to the Shakers both a way to express their inner devotion and an outward sign of their special grace. Work was sacred – and not just any work, but work done to the utmost skill and energy of the worker. Perfection in work reflected a perfection of spirit.

One of mother Ann's most oft-quoted admonitions was: "Do your work as though it were to last a thousand years and you were to die tomorrow."

Thus, when the Shakers made an object, even though it was strictly utilitarian (they didn't believe in superfluous decoration or display), the object had to be pure in design and execution. They particularly prized hand work, such as turning wood or weaving cloth, and

until late in their history they strove for self-sufficiency by making as many of the objects of routine life as possible – but all to the standard of perfection.

This dedication to doing the everyday things as well as possible carried over into the Shaker attitudes toward farming and manufacture. During their decades of greatest success – the mid-1800s – most of the Shaker settlements were thriving examples of the best of pre-industrial American agriculture. They had good land, they cared for it exceptionally well, and they strove ever to improve their technique. In addition, the Shakers had an abundance of skillful labor to lavish on the land.

They also numbered among themselves many clever and innovative people who were ingenious at devising well-engineered and beautifully-made labor-saving devices. The list of Shaker inventions is long and impressive, and even today their gadgets seem to be inspired.

The Shakers also used the available labor to make products that the outside world was happy to pay for. Various Shaker villages developed thriving trades in high-class seeds, herbs and herb medicines, brooms, baskets, cooperage, and many other extremely well-made and useful items. One was assured of first-class goods when buying from the Shaker Trustees, and their reputation stood high all over the land.

By the mid-19th century there were more than 5000 Shakers living in organized societies, owning communally as many as 60,000 acres of land. The members were industrious and free from want. Among the villages were many children, usually brought into the societies by converted parents or adopted by the Shakers as orphans (children were always allowed free choice to stay or leave after reaching maturity). Shakers were renowned for their good health and long lives. The daily routines of work were punctuated by the emotional release of worship services that still preserved the strange shaking and utterings of the first Shakers, but had been refined into more formal dancing and singing exercises.

For the truly committed Shaker, it was a satisfying life, limited perhaps in the perspective of outsiders, but without the tension and anxiety that goes with the need to make daily choices. Shaker faith was based on offbeat doctrines, but it resulted in a harmonious simplicity.

The Shaker way of life, of course, contained

within itself the seed of destruction. No society built on celibacy could survive if ever the original wellspring of inspiration ran dry. So it is not remarkable that the Shaker world eventually began to dwindle; what amazes is the long run of the Shakers as a viable community. Until very late in the 19th century, Shakers still attracted converts, although in nothing like the numbers of the 1820s and '30s.

The Civil War marked the beginning of the long, slow decline, and as the nation turned over the ensuing decades to become more industrial and urban rather than agricultural and rural, the fortunes of the Shakers suffered. Theirs was a pre-eminently agrarian way of life. Although they were industrious and successful in small scale manufacture, it is hard to imagine a smoke-belching, urban Shaker factory. As farming began to lose its central place in the American economy, the attractions of the Shaker life began to fade.

Ever so slowly, the villages began to wither away. The average age of the Shaker population grew progressively older, and few came forward to replace elderly Shakers as they passed on. More and more, the villages had to pay hired hands to work the fields and tend the livestock. The abundant laborers who had powered Shaker prosperity disappeared.

By the beginning of the 20th century, it was clear that the end of a meaningful Shaker presence was at hand. One by one, the villages began to shut down. Whitewater, Watervliet, and Union Village in Ohio disappeared. Pleasant Hill in Kentucky was signed over to worldly interests, soon to be followed by South Union. Most of the New England villages suffered the same fates, with the rapidly-decreasing numbers of believers consolidating forces in fewer and fewer places, until only four Shaker societies were left after World War II.

In 1947, New Lebanon, which had been the center of Shaker organization for 160 years, ceased to function as a living settlement, and the central authority was transferred to Canterbury, New Hampshire.

Yet Shakers never quite disappeared altogether. A few sisters – most of them brought into the societies as orphans – hung on to the old ways. Canterbury persisted, as did the physically-isolated settlement at Sabbathday Lake, Maine. Much of the spirit was gone, however, and the elderly sisters of Canterbury decreed that no new recruits could be accepted, even though naive flower children seeking an easy enlightenment often turned up on the Shakers' doorsteps during the 1960s.

Although their numbers were few also, the sisters at Sabbathday Lake were on the average younger than those at Canterbury and somewhat more open-minded. For several years they allowed two or three earnest admirers to live and work closely with the surviving community. When, in the 1980s, the eldresses of Canterbury relented, the Sabbathday Lake Shakers admitted three men as the first new Shaker converts in decades.

It is therefore quite wrong to speak of the Shakers completely in the past tense. While no one seriously contemplates a resurgence of Shakerdom in America, there are, in fact, Shakers still in the land, living communally, cultivating their herbs, worshipping with Shaker song and dance, and preserving a link to the religious inspirations received by Mother Ann so long ago. There is enough vitality in the Sabbathday Lake Shaker community to make it impossible to write the end of the Shakers' tale just yet.

And, no matter what the condition of modern Shakerdom, there is abundant attention paid to the Shaker past. Many of the former Shaker villages now welcome visitors to a vision of times gone by. Pleasant Hill, for example, after 50 years out of Shaker ownership, was purchased by a non-profit corporation in the 1960s and returned to beautiful condition, serving now as a living history museum. The Hancock Shaker Village in Massachusetts passed immediately from Shaker ownership to a restoration group, and its famous Round Stone Barn symbolizes New England Shakers for many tourists each year. Even the last two remaining living Shaker communities at Canterbury and Sabbathday Lake entertain summer visitors. Almost every former Shaker site has at least a museum, displaying the images and artifacts of the believers. So it is that after two centuries that we are able to glimpse at least part of the heritage of Shaker harmony.

The Shaker story is both strange and compelling, the tale of an intense religious doctrine that eventually burned itself out, leaving us to admire and puzzle over the artifacts of its belief.

The Shaker settlement at New Lebanon, N.Y., founded in 1787, was the first permanent "gathering" of Shakers into a separate community. New Lebanon (the name changed to Mt. Lebanon in 1861) also became the center of the Shaker Ministry: its Elders and Eldresses directed general policies for all Shakers everywhere. Today, the Mt. Lebanon buildings house a private preparatory school, but the village is open to visitors during part of the year. A small museum (facing page top) is located in the Wash House. The principal buildings (previous pages) were used during Shaker times by the Church Family. Left to right are the first Meeting House (one of the earliest built by Shakers), the Trustees Office, and the large second Meeting House (also pictured below), completed in 1824, with an unusual arched roof designed to provide unobstructed floor space for Shaker dancing during services. Shaker barns (right and overleaf) were central to their agricultural way of life.

THE SHAKERS
HERE ESTABLISHED, 1787,
FIRST COMMUNITY IN AMERICA.
A CELIBATE ORDER DEVOTED TO
"HANDS TO WORK-HEARTS TO GOD"

ERECTED 1960

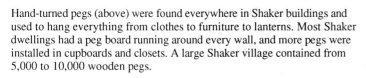
Hand-turned pegs (above) were found everywhere in Shaker buildings and used to hang everything from clothes to furniture to lanterns. Most Shaker dwellings had a peg board running around every wall, and more pegs were installed in cupboards and closets. A large Shaker village contained from 5,000 to 10,000 wooden pegs.

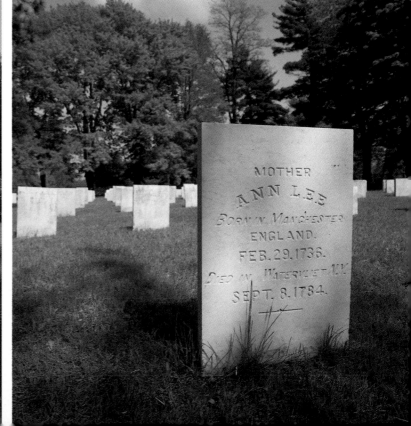

The Shaker commercial seed industry (facing page top), begun at Mt. Lebanon (facing page bottom left) in the 1790s, was the sect's most successful business enterprise. Watervliet, N.Y., (then called Niskeyuna) was a dismal frontier swamp when Mother Ann Lees and her handful of first Shakers arrived in the 1770s. Until her death in 1784, she used the crude settlement as her home base for mission trips that ranged throughout New England. Mother Ann's grave is in the Watervliet cemetery (facing page bottom right). The surviving Shaker leaders organized Watervliet as a communal village in 1787, and it continued until 1938. The site was nearly obliterated in this century by construction of the nearby Albany County Airport, but the cemetery and the Meeting House (left) are open to the public. The benches in the Meeting House were for "wordly" visitors from the outside, who were usually allowed to observe Shaker worship services. Pictured below is the Ministry.

The Shaker Museum at Old Chatham, N.Y., while not an original Shaker site, is the largest collection of Shaker objects – more than 32,000 items – gathered from many Shaker villages and representing 200 years of Shaker history. Interpretive displays include everyday things such as cloaks and buckets and examples of Shaker furniture such as the cherry-wood wardrobe from Pleasant Hill, Ky., (previous page). Oval boxes and carriers (facing page) were characteristic Shaker products: ingeniously designed and meticulously constructed. The medicine room (above) displays crocks, sieves, and bottles on a long "herb" table. The copper-tanked fire engine (left) was built at Canterbury, N.H., in 1822. Tools in the wood-working shop (overleaf) were run by belts from overhead water- or steam-powered shafts.

A kitchen pantry (facing page) displays a variety of cooking utensils and tools. Shakers ate communally, and the kitchen sisters needed to prepare large quantities of food for each meal, so they relied extensively on labor-saving devices for processing fresh ingredients. The furniture gallery (left) includes a clock originally built by Benjamin Youngs at Watervliet, N.Y., about 1800. The Shaker chairs are perhaps the most famous of the sect's furniture designs, along with the severe but well-proportioned benches, such as this one from Enfield, N.H. The "sage pounder" from Hancock, Mass. (below on right) was a water-powered, rotating wooden cylinder used to process plants for the Shakers' highly successful dried and medicinal herb trade. As the cylinder turned, iron balls inside ground up the dried plants.

Several display rooms at Old Chatham show furniture, tools, and utensils in typical Shaker settings. The dining room (facing page top) features a set of china from the Hancock, Mass. settlement. At the rear is a large pine cabinet-on-chest from the North Family dining room at Watervliet. The alignment of wood-burning stoves and implements (facing page bottom) signifies the Shakers' use of iron stoves to heat virtually all their dwellings. They discovered early on that stoves were much more efficient and cleaner than traditional methods, so they designed and built small stoves capable of heating an entire room. Few Shaker buildings had fireplaces. An agricultural shed (above) shows farming tools of all kinds: wooden grain shovels, two-prong hay forks, buckets and baskets, and grain cradles (hanging on wall). The special orchard ladders were tapered toward the top for easy work in fruit trees. The Deacon's Office (left) features a display of roofing tools.

The Shakers of Canterbury, N.H., enjoyed great commercial success in making and selling 19th-century washing machines. The one shown here (right) has two compartments with wooden agitators. The machine, believed to date from 1860, was water powered. The Shakers didn't invent the power washing machine, but purchased rights to an early design and improved it, eventually patenting the changes. Also seen in the laundry room are drying racks and a large press at the rear, used to finish napkins and other flat linens. A collection of kitchen implements (facing page top) includes a sugar mill, a flour sifter, a copper kettle, and a butter churn. The built-in pine cupboard at the rear is a design typical of the Hancock and Mt. Lebanon Shakers. The bed (below right) from Pleasant Hill, like most Shaker beds, features rollers so it may be pulled sideways from the wall for cleaning underneath.

In addition to woodworking shops (left), all Shaker villages had blacksmithing shops (facing page). Shown here are a variety of metalworking tools, including an overhead bellows. The handcart (below) was used at Canterbury to carry hot meals to workers in the field. Note also the gravestones, which later Shakers frowned on and often removed from earlier cemeteries and put to use as utilitarian slabs of stone. Overleaf left: historical photos of 20th-century Shaker sisters from Canterbury demonstrate a variety of tasks. Early Shakers banned photography or painting, but by the 1900s most Shakers had embraced the modern camera and many were enthusiastic amateur photographers. A U.S. patent (overleaf right) from the Old Chatham collections registered improvements to a water wheel by a Shaker of Enfield, N.H. On the following pages are day books from Enfield, Conn. Shakers were compulsive recordkeepers.

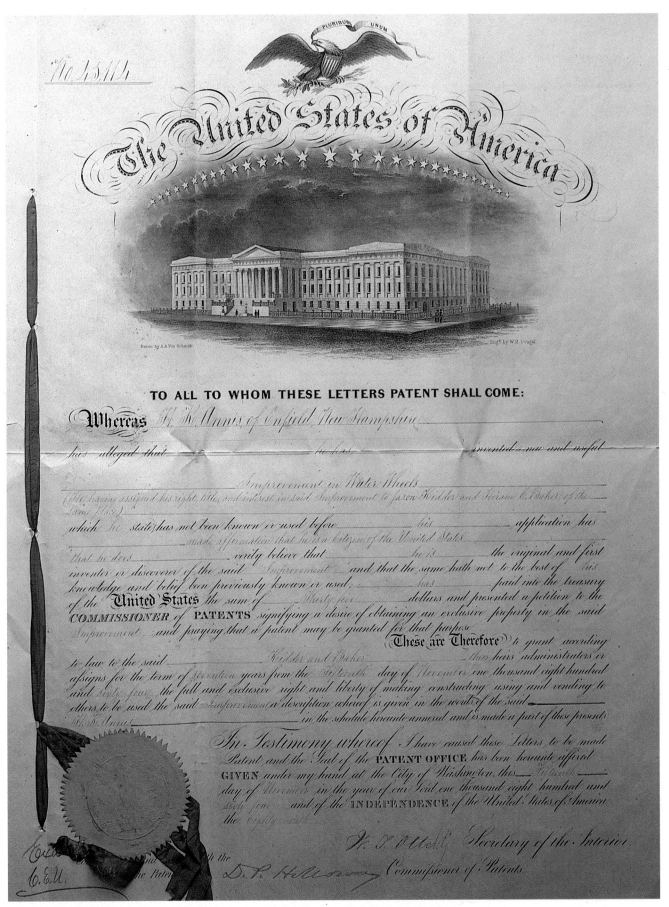

All photographs these pages and overleaf courtesy The Shaker Museum, Old Chatham, New York.

...t long
pump

...oak Bottoms at...

...to one Bushel Cor...

...Shewing your horse

...Shewing your horse

...ing Dr to Shewing your horse

...King Dr To Shewing your ho...

...ul Mills Dr to making Fore Barrels one hay...

...der and hooping Barrel

By Cash Two Dollars

...Rhodes Billings Dr to two $6 & 10 Cut...

Benjamin King Dr to minding a hay fork...

ary
6 1803
31   Benjamin King Dr to Shewing horse

Samuel King Dr to Shewing horse

March 18   Jerah Mills Dr to mending Chairs

April 11   Hosea King Dr to mantle trees and or
To two Cranges

June
the 9
1803   Jesse Richason Dr to Two Bushe...
of rye at fore Shillings a Bush...

Hosea King Dr to making...
a Crane   14

Date		Description	£	s	d
June 24 1803		Samuel Mills Dr to a braking up plow to Plow two acres	0	9	0
1st		William Mills Dr to making 2 barrels Sider at our mill	0	2	6
Oct		Benjamin King Dr to making 2 hands of Sider	0	2	0
Nov		to making a bucher Knife	0	1	0
		to Sawing Brought brom the Saw Book 1803	0	12	8
25		to Sawing 222 fet Slitwork	0	3	5
Dec		Josiah Blaget Dr to a horse Collar	0	18	0
		to a horse yoak Irond	0	13	6
		to leather for neck Collar	3	2	0
Feb 1804 6		Benjamin Pierce Dr to a Loome	1	6	0
		To a Quill wheel	0	8	0
Jenuary 1807		Benjamin King Dr payd to Boze Terry	0	4	6
		to new laying a brode axe	0	5	6
		Brought from the Saw Book 1804	2	10	6
			0	10	0
June 9 1804		for a barryl of Sider	4	15	5
April 14 1806		Jesse Richabon Dr for one hondred one quarter at one shilling nine pence a hondred	0	2	2
		for half a bushel ot wheat	0	1	6
may 1809		Samuel King Dr to potatoes	0	4	6
		to 74 lb of Rye kernell	0	8	6
Sept		to half bushel of seed wheat	0	6	0
		to half bushel of peaches	0	2	0
Novem		to one bushel of wheat	0	12	0
		to six lb of wheat flower at 6 cents a lb	0	5	6
Jenuary 1810		to Beef	0	1	6
April 11		to hay ½ hundred	0	9	0
Cr Sept		Samuel King by 2 Days work thrashing oats			
		by one Days work at the quara			

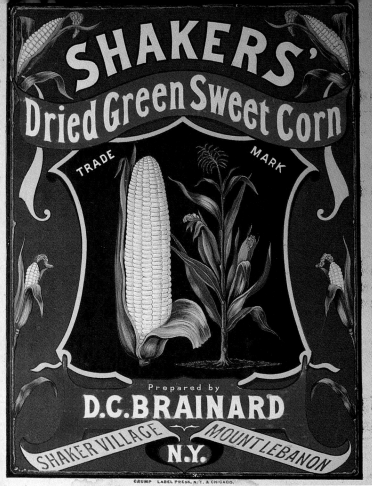

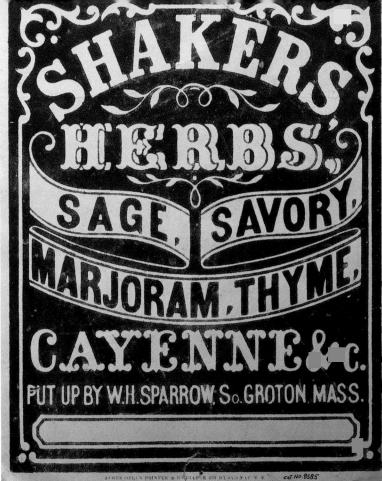

The Shakers marketed wholesome processed foods during the 19th century, when typical commercial canning was unsanitary and unsafe. These labels and advertisements, including one for the famous Shaker apple sauce, are from the Old Chatham collections. *(Photographs courtesy The Shaker Museum, Old Chatham, New York.)*

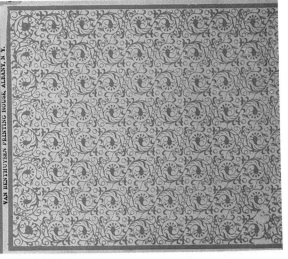

PACKED IN SANITARY CANS

ANNA CASE, Trustee

BUTTER BEANS.

FIRST QUALITY.
CONTENTS 20 OUNCES

FRESH TOMATOES.

FIRST QUALITY.
CONTENTS 2 POUNDS

SHAKERS'
HERMETICALLY SEALED
VEGETABLES.

ANNA CASE, Trustee
SOUTH FAMILY, SHAKERS,
West Albany, R. F. D.

SHAKERS,

STRING BEANS.

PACKED BY THE SHAKERS

ADDRESS,
D. C. Brainard,
MOUNT LEBANON,
COL. CO., N. Y.

AT MOUNT LEBANON, N. Y.

41

Along with Shaker objects (facing page and below left) the Shaker Museum at Old Chatham includes rare images such as the photograph of Elder Henry Blinn (left), Canterbury's most prominent leader and an articulate spokesman for the Shakers, whose activities included writing, editing, printing, botany, bee-keeping, and dentistry. Below is a view of a schoolroom at Canterbury and bottom is a portrait of Canterbury Sister Emma Neal. Sister Cora Sarle's watercolors (overleaf) are lovely illustrations of Canterbury during the early part of this century. *(Photographs these pages and overleaf courtesy The Shaker Museum, Old Chatham, New York.)*

#11,952 Water cblor 3½ x 5½
by Sr. C[ora] H. S[arle].

"West Entrance to Large Barn,
                    Shakers, N.H."

West Entrance to Large Barn. Shaker N.H.

#8034 Water color by
Sister Cora Helena Sarle of
Canterbury, N.H. Shakers

b. Feb. 18, 1867
d. March 1956
Painted in 1955

"Ministrys Dwelling, Shakers, N.H."

Ministrys Dwelling. Shaker. N.H.

#8035 Water color
by Sr. Cora Helena Sarle
of Canterbury, N.H. Shakers

b. Feb. 18, 1867
d. March 1956
Painted in 1954

"Church Lane, Shakers"

Church Lane Shaker N.H

44

East Canterbury Shaker Church, Built 1792. N.H.

9796
G

#8032 Water color by
Sr. Cora Helena Sarle
of Canterbury, N.H. Shakers
b. Feb. 18, 1867
d. March 1956

Painted in 1954-55.

"West entrance to large barn"

West enterance to large Barn. Shakers. N.H.

9796
G

#8033 Watercolor by
Sr. Cora Helena Sarle
of Canterbury, N.H. Shakers
b. Feb. 18, 1867
d. March 1956

Painted in 1955.

"Oldest House in Shaker Hill"

Oldest House on Shaker Hill. Shakers. N.H.

The Shakers, who loved to travel, were enthusiastic about the advent of the automobile. Most Eastern shaker villages bought cars for communal use. The photos (facing page) show sisters from Canterbury on a visit in the early 1900s to Sabbathday Lake, Maine. *(Collection of the United Society of Shakers, Sabbathday Lake, Maine.)* Below is a wagon shed, moved from Canterbury, N.H., that now houses a Shaker Museum at Shelburne, Vt. The re-created bedroom (left) contains furniture from Canterbury.

Shakertown at Pleasant Hill, Ky., was one of the prosperous western Shaker villages that dotted Ohio and Kentucky. Shaker missionaries to Kentucky from the East arrived in 1805 in the midst of an intense, prolonged religious revival movement, and they successfully converted key leaders to Shakerdom. The Shakers of Pleasant Hill occupied a beautiful location on the edge of the fertile Kentucky Bluegrass region, near to the Kentucky River, and eventually amassed nearly 5,000 acres of prime farm land. At its peak, Pleasant Hill was home to almost 500 Shakers. The main building is the 40-room Centre Family Dwelling (above, right, and facing page top), whose massive limestone walls and careful construction testify to Shaker craftsmanship. Restoration of Pleasant Hill began in the early 1960s and resulted in an impressive, carefully re-created agricultural Shaker village. Twenty-seven buildings have been restored, and the site includes more than 2,000 acres of land.

48

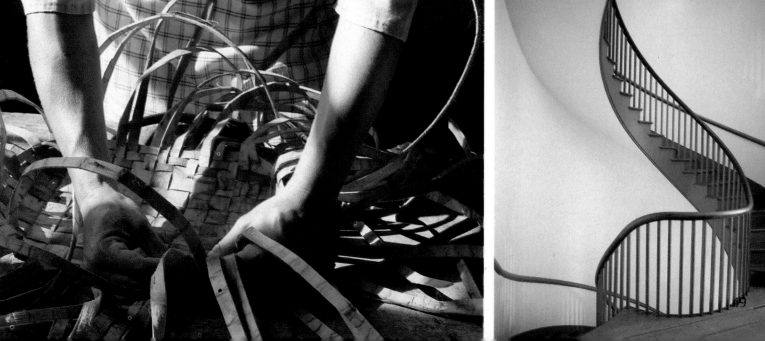

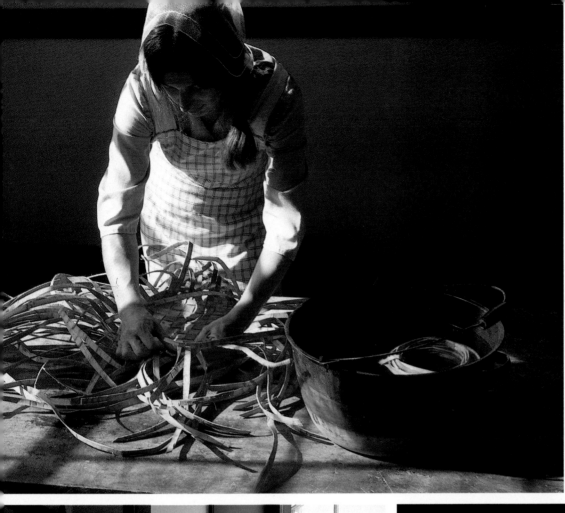

The Centre Family Dwelling (facing page top) is open to tours, and some of the Pleasant Hill buildings such as the East Family Dwelling (facing page bottom) have been converted to accommodate overnight guests in rooms furnished with Shaker-style furniture. The site also features Shaker-style public dining in the former Trustees Office building, whose graceful spiral stairway is shown on the previous page (bottom right). In other buildings, costumed interpreters re-create Shaker crafts. Basketmaking, for example, was an important activity that fulfilled a basic utilitarian need. In Kentucky, baskets were often woven from willow strips that had first been soaked in water to make them pliable (left and previous page). The basket hanging in the window of the Centre Dwelling (below left) was a special design for use in gathering herbs and vegetables: it was curved on one side to hang snugly against the hip. The Shaker-made sieve (below) was for sorting seeds.

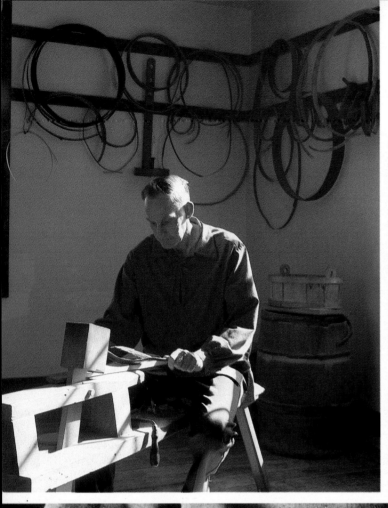

In the Pleasant Hill Shaker community there was less emphasis on manufacture for sale and more on making tools for immediate use in farming and daily rural life. In the Cooper's Shop (page 58 top), brothers turned out barrels, buckets, and all sizes of wooden containers. Shown left is an interpretive craftsman hand-planing staves, making both wooden (bottom) and metal (below) hoops, and finishing a water dipper (facing page).

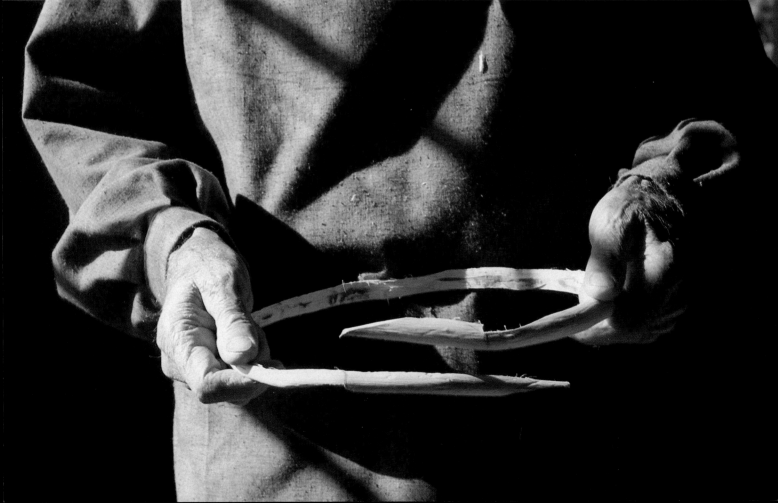

One of the profitable Shaker activities was the manufacture of brooms. An eastern Shaker brother had invented the flat broom, an efficient improvement on the traditional round style, and Shaker communities everywhere grew broom corn (right) for this essential household item. The Shakers at South Union in Western Kentucky produced up to 150,000 brooms yearly. Shaker emphasis on wholesome food may seem today merely a source of interesting Early American recipes, but at the time when the Shaker societies were formed, very few average Americans knew how to prepare nutritious meals. Shaker kitchen sisters developed communal cooking in harmony with Shaker principles, using only the best ingredients (such as the blackberries shown below right) and preparing balanced meals simply but well. The Shakers were also interested in herbal medicine and developed a successful trade in dried herbs (overleaf left) and such specialties as rose water made from dried petals (overleaf right).

For much of their history Shakers strove to be as self-sufficient as possible. Until relatively late in the 1800s, Shaker villages grew and made nearly everything they needed for daily life, including the cloth for their distinctive style of dress. The Shakers of Pleasant Hill raised sheep from which they sheared the wool and produced excellent material after a long routine of processing. The raw wool was colored with natural dyes (facing page), then carded and spun (overleaf), often on large "walking" spinning wheels. The finished yarn (following pages) was ready for weaving or knitting. Kentucky Shakers were unique in producing of an even finer grade of fabric: silk. The mild climate allowed Shakers at both Pleasant Hill and South Union successfully to raise silk worms. The resulting material was usually sewn into silk scarves which were often sent to eastern Shaker societies as much-prized mementos of western Shakerdom. The Pleasant Hill sisters also made linen from home-grown flax.

The restored Centre Family Dwelling at Pleasant Hill (left), with its double entryways – one for women and one for men – gives visitors a striking impression of the sense of proportion Shaker builders incorporated into their living places. Shaker routine was regimented and probably filled with a certain kind of tension resulting from the strict separation of the sexes, but the interior spaces of the Centre Family Dwelling (facing page) exude a harmony of dimension combined with gentle, diffused natural light that must have done much to soothe the irritations of communal life. The building was constructed under the supervision of a young Shaker, Micajah Burnett, and generally patterned after eastern Shaker buildings. The exterior walls are of thick limestone blocks, and the plain interior is delicately finished in natural and painted woods. Some of the original paint from the early 19th century remains, despite five decades of disuse between the closing of Pleasant Hill as a living Shaker community and its restoration. Below is the East Family Brethren Shop.

The Shaker art in cabinetry is illustrated by a storage area for linens in the Centre Family Dwelling (top). Shown facing page are shoemaking tools and forms (hanging on wall) used to fit each member of the society individually with footwear.

The Shaker desire for order led them to follow a regimented daily schedule. They rose before dawn and, after kneeling in prayer, they dressed and proceeded to breakfast. At Pleasant Hill, they marched silently down the Centre Family Dwelling hallway, women on one side, men on the other, through the double doors (above) to the dining room. After the meal, the brothers went to work in the fields and shops, while the sisters cleaned, cooked, and saw to domestic tasks. Every room was cleaned every day. Dinner was at noon, followed by more work hours until supper. The evenings were given to study, meetings, and worship. All retired at the same time to simple sleeping rooms, such as the brothers' room (left). Those who were ill moved into special infirmary rooms (facing page).

69

The Meeting House at Pleasant Hill (facing page top) was simple, spacious, and well-lighted, similar in style to most of the wooden frame buildings in the village. Even the structures housing the water system and bath houses (top) were carefully proportioned. The broad green spaces around buildings were often planted to herb gardens (above and left).

These pages: views of the Centre Family Dwelling at Pleasant Hill. One thing the Shakers never lacked during the mid-1800s was an abundant supply of labor, which their ordered way of life converted to an astounding productivity. The East Family Sisters of Pleasant Hill recorded in 1844: "A General View of the work done this year besides the weaving. 70 pairs linen trousers and 26 pairs cloth trousers, 40 cotton gowns and 40 winter gowns, 13 drab cloaks, and 24 bonnets, 68 caps, 24 hats for brethren, 3 great coats, 31 jackets, 9 frocks, 80 shirts. Spun 198 run of flax, and 248 of worsted." All this was in addition to cooking, cleaning, caring for the sick, and other routine chores.

The layout of the main village at Pleasant Hill was careful but uncrowded. Shakers seem to have been particularly sensitive to the effect of space and the relationship between buildings. The current restored village reflects the settlement at its height in the mid-1800s. The entire original site, however, covered a much larger surrounding area, including earlier mills and log structures on nearby Shawnee Run Creek. The original mill sites were recently acquired by the non-profit restoration corporation, and plans are underway to rebuild and replicate buildings that formed the earliest Pleasant Hill industries: a cloth mill, sawmill, gristmill and linseed oil mill. When completed, the additional site will show visitors another side of Shaker life.

Sabbathday Lake, Maine (top), still home to a handful of Shakers, is the last vital bastion of the living Shaker tradition. It is part working community, part research center, and part place to visit. The Meeting House (above) and the Herb House, Boys Shop, and Wood House (facing page top) mix with still-used barns (facing page bottom).

76

Founded in 1794, Sabbathday Lake (formerly called New Gloucester) was one of the smaller permanent Shaker settlements and somewhat isolated. As the Shaker population in general dwindled nearly to the point of disappearance, a few active Shakers remained at Sabbathday. By careful consolidation of resources (and a more modest establishment to begin with) the Sabbathday community continued as a viable gathering. The last brother died in 1961, but under orders from Canterbury, N.H., the remaining sisters of Sabbathday were unable to accept new members until recently, when three men were allowed formally to affiliate. The Sabbathday settlement presents a sharp contrast to the pristine restorations of Pleasant Hill, Ky., and Hancock, Mass. The sheep in the fields and barns are not mere ornaments, but part of a still-active farm. Visitors are welcomed throughout summer weekdays, but are not allowed to impinge on the community's continuing practice of the Shaker way of life.

Canterbury, N.H., is also a living Shaker community, but the Shaker population has been reduced to three very elderly sisters. Most of the site has been turned over to a non-profit corporation that maintains the buildings and conducts tours for the public. Canterbury, founded in 1792, gathered around 300 members at its peak. Twenty-two buildings remain, and six are open to the public. Shown here are the laundry (top), the Brethren Shop (left), the Creamery (above), a carriage house (facing page top), and the Ministry Shop (facing page bottom).

Many of the implements of everyday life and much of the furniture have been removed from Canterbury and are now found in other Shaker museums and collections. The buildings, however, provide a look at both the traditions of the Shakers and how continuing communities adapted to changing times. The laundry (facing page and left) still has wooden forms for blocking knitted socks and a large brick stove to heat water for the work of washing mounds of dirty clothes. The rather mundane buildings shown below, seemingly un-Shakerlike in appearance, illustrate adaption – the tower is part of a garage for the first Canterbury horseless carriage. In 1910, a Canterbury brother built the powerhouse (foreground) and wired the entire village for electricity supplied by a steam generator and batteries, making Canterbury one of the first electrified villages in the region.

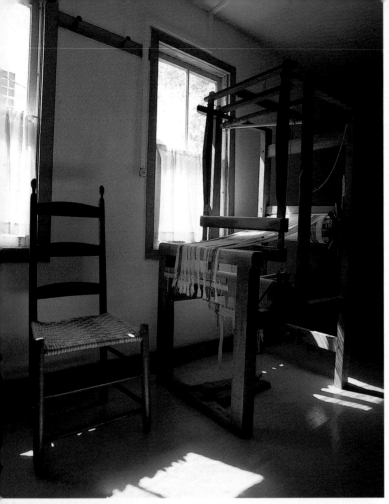

Shown above are a loom (top left) in the Sisters Shop and the dentistry shop (right). Canterbury's best-known leader, Elder Henry Blinn, was also a dentist, and he built the bureau in his bedroom in the Ministry Shop (left). Above is a sitting room in the Sisters Shop. Facing page are the Dwelling House (top) and the Brethren Shop (bottom).

At its height, Canterbury was a thriving community, laid out in regular order over a large area. When Elder Henry Blinn mapped the Center Family in 1848, his diagram showed 71 buildings, gardens, barns, and farm pens. Of the surviving buildings, the laundry shows a clever set of sliding racks (right) for drying wet clothes, long ironing tables (facing page top) and a steam-powered laundry press (facing page bottom left). The Sisters Shop (below and facing page bottom right) still exhibits examples of Shaker furniture, such as the double sewing cabinets. The pictures on the walls further indicate this is a long-lived Shaker community, since earlier Shaker doctrine forbade such displays. The 1860 *Rules and Orders for the Church* admonished: "No maps, Charts, Pictures nor paintings, should ever be hung up in retiring rooms; and no pictures, paintings or likenesses, as Daguerreotypes etc. should ever be kept by Believers."

Shown above are the North Shop and syrup shop. Most of the New England Shaker villages gathered and sold maple syrup as a regular part of the fall routine. Right is the laundry, and facing page bottom is the Creamery and the North Shop, with the powerhouse in the background. A schoolhouse (facing page top) was a standard fixture of most Shaker villages. Surprisingly for a celibate sect, most Shaker communities were home for many children, who were brought in by converted parents or who were lodged with the Shakers as orphans or wards. Individual brothers took charge of the boys and sisters took charge of the girls. The Shakers provided a good general education in addition to religious instruction, but all children were allowed to choose between the Shakers and the world when they reached maturity. The surviving sisters at Canterbury, for example, were adopted as orphans.

"Chosen Vale," the Shaker settlement at Enfield, N.H., on the shores of Lake Mascoma, was only middling size as Shaker villages went, but it boasted the largest single Shaker building, the Great Stone Dwelling (facing page). Finished in 1841, it stands as imposing and sturdy as the day the last stone was laid – four full stories and two half-stories, with row after row of windows. The Enfield Shaker settlement closed in 1923, when the few remaining Shakers moved to Canterbury, and the property was deeded to the Roman Catholic Order of LaSalette. The site is now open to the public for tours of buildings and a small museum.

Shakers needed many agricultural buildings to house their large herds of livestock, and when planning barns, they tended to use the natural advantages of the site very cleverly. The wooden barn at Enfield (facing page bottom) was typically built into the side of a hill to provide a natural ramp to the second story. Reproduction Shaker furniture in a craftsman's shop at Enfield (this page) testifies to the demand for Shaker designs. The Enfield museum (overleaf) includes displays on other Shaker settlements, including Hancock, Mass.

93

HANCOCK, MASSACHUSETTS Top, Church Family Main Dwelling House (Baldwin, 1939). Left, cupboard (Boucher, 1962). Above, dining room doors (Pearson, 1968). Below left, interior (Boucher, 1962). Below right, bake oven (Boucher, 1962).

"All are required to rise in the morning at the signal given for that purpose; and when any rise before the usual time they must not be noisy.... No one should lean back against the wall, bed, or ceiling of dwelling rooms. It is also wrong to sit with the feet on the rounds of chairs.... All who sleep in a room must go to bed at the same time, and together, if not prevented by other duties.... All should retire to rest in the fear of God, without any playing, or boisterous laughing, and lie straight."

Millennial Laws

HANCOCK
left and
(Winter,
Meetingho
(Boucher,
detail (Bo
(Pearson,

"All shoul
of God wa
abreast if
ciently wid
together, a
talking, la
railing, wh
meeting...
place them
for the w
should be
right and
back: forwa
as long as
should ther
it has a ten
Brethren a
themselves
meeting."

Little of the Shaker village at Harvard, Mass. survives at the original site, although the early Shaker cemetery (facing page top) remains, as does the house (right) where Mother Ann was reputed to have lived during her long missionary sojourn in Harvard. Several of the original buildings now stand at nearby Fruitlands Museum (above, top and facing page bottom).

The Fruitlands Museum recounts the history of two communal societies: one experimental and short-lived, the other fundamental and successful. The museum is located on the site of an attempt at secular communal living by a group of New England intellectuals (the Transcendentalists), which failed miserably. In 1914, Clara Endicott Sears of Boston purchased the derelict Fruitlands house, and because she was interested in the Shakers, she bought a wooden house from them when the Harvard Society dissolved in 1918, moved the Shaker building to the Fruitlands location, and started a museum. Overleaf: the Round Stone Barn at Hancock Shaker Village in Massachusetts is perhaps the best-known Shaker building in New England, visited and photographed by thousands each year. It is the focal point of the restored and maintained "City of Peace," founded in 1790. When the Shakers gave up the village in 1960, it passed immediately to a non-profit corporation to become a living museum of Shaker life. The location in the Berkshires adds to the attraction.

The Round Barn, a marvel of efficient Shaker design, was built in 1826. It burned to the stone walls in 1864 and was rebuilt with the addition of a new circular pit basement. The wooden third story was added in the 1880s. The final plan made it a vertically-integrated factory for dairy farming. Hay and fodder were carted to the upper level directly from elevated ramps and stored or pitched down to the central haymow. The dairy cattle were stabled on the main level and held by stanchions to be fed and milked. The manure was scooped through trapdoors to the lower level pit to be shoveled out for fertilizer. The circular design allowed one Shaker herdsman to work from the middle to feed all the animals with a minimum of pitching and hauling of fodder. Two hundred and seventy feet in circumference, the barn could accommodate 52 head of cattle and two span of horses, with room for 300 tons of hay.

The Brick Dwelling House at Hancock (previous pages and facing page top) was built in 1830 along typical Shaker lines, with thick walls, many windows, and dual, separate entrances. It contained living and work space for 100 Shaker brothers and sisters as well as specialty rooms. The sewing room (above) features a sewing cabinet with a large work top for spreading material, and drawers on two sides for access by several workers at once. The brothers' retiring room (right) shows the typical spare neatness of Shaker living, with brooms, a boot puller and individual towels hung out of the way on pegs. The Deacon's Office (facing page bottom) now displays lovely examples of Shaker furniture and a hanging key board. The Hancock Shaker Village was unique in passing directly from Shaker hands to museum status. When the Shakers decided to close the settlement in 1960, after 170 years, a group of neighbors organized themselves to take over the site. The country's foremost authority on Shakerdom, Edward Deming Andrews, was the first curator. Eldress Emma B. King of the Canterbury Ministry spoke on behalf of the Shakers when the property was transferred:

"The Parent Ministry has always been especially anxious that these lands and buildings be devoted to some use which is charitable or educational and of benefit to the community..." The Hancock museum fulfills this charge with careful restoration and maintenance, tours of the site's buildings, and a busy summer schedule of interpretive and educational activities.

The Brick Dwelling House at Hancock Village displays outstanding examples of Shaker furniture and room style – two features of Shaker life that attract considerable present-day admiration. The side-by-side double desk in the Elders' Room (facing page top left) is lovely in detail and practical as a space saver. The rocking chair and cupboard (facing page top right) are in the same exhibit. The meeting room in the Brick Dwelling House (above) is a striking illustration of the Shaker love of simplicity and spareness. When hundreds of Shakers lived at Hancock during the 19th century, such a plain style contrasted very sharply to prevailing notions of interior decoration. Most American and British homes were dense with overstuffed furniture, lace antimacassars, bric-a-brac, and brocaded curtains. Victorians, such as British writer Charles Dickens who visited the New England Shakers, found bare Shaker rooms distasteful and unpleasant. Modern eyes tend more to see beauty in the simple forms.

Even the Shaker work areas were cleanly designed and equipped. The pharmacy in the Brick Dwelling House (previous pages) might have been a place of clutter but for the organized Shaker built-in cupboard, the ubiquitous pegboards, and the functional work surfaces. The same is true for the sewing room (these pages). Overleaf: An interpreter at Hancock Village cards and spins wool.

Top: Shaker clay-bowl pipes with wooden stems, (above) scrub brushes drying in the kitchen window of the Brick Dwelling House, (facing page top) the kitchen of the Brick Dwelling House, and (right and facing page bottom) the Nurses Shop or infirmary of the Brick Dwelling House. The adult-size cradles were for soothing patients.

The combination Machine Shop and
Laundry at Hancock (left, below and
facing page top) has been altered over
the years since the first part of the
structure was built in 1790. Note the
long run of exposed stovepipe, a
device Shakers used extensively to
radiate extra heat into rooms. The barn
complex (facing page bottom) includes
some of the more recent Hancock
buildings. The original barn was put
up in 1880, burned to the ground in
1910 following a lightning strike, but
was re-built thereafter. The Shakers
followed their usual practice and took
advantage of natural slopes to provide
easy access to the upper levels. The
buildings currently house
woodworking and herb processing.

Originally, power for the Machine Shop (facing page) came from an overshot water wheel. The Hancock Shakers built a reservoir on the nearby mountainside to provide water for the wheel. The laundry (this page) required a good deal of cooperage and many simply constructed wooden drying racks. Washing clothes consumed a great deal of labor in early Shaker times, but the same doctrines that impelled Shaker sisters to sweep and dust every room every day also instructed them to replace soiled cloths and linens immediately with freshly laundered goods.

The Hancock Schoolhouse (facing page) is a recent reconstruction of the original 1820 building. The wood shed and the pile of split firewood (above) are reminders of the labor necessary to provide energy during the winter for the dozens of Shaker stoves. The brothers typically worked throughout the fall months to cut, haul, and split hardwood, which was stacked and seasoned in huge quantities. The frame in the yard next to the Sister Shop (left) was for dipping candles. Most Shaker buildings were lit by candles until the mid-1800s, when they switched over to oil lanterns. Eventually most of the buildings were electrified.

The Meeting House (interior shown below) originally stood at Shirley, Mass. and was identical to the Hancock Meeting House which was torn down by the Shakers in 1938. Chairs were perhaps the best-known Shaker furniture, made and sold widely by the Shakers until the 20th century. At Hancock Village, craftsmen produce reproduction chairs to Shaker patterns, using Shaker tools (facing page and overleaf). The chairs varied slightly from maker to maker and village to village, but they shared a distinctive and immediately recognizable design. As usual with Shaker-made objects, the chairs were unadorned, strong, practical, and elegant in simple concept. They were also extremely well made. In chair design, as in nearly all aspects of life, the Shakers believed that "every force evolves a form."